3/15 $17

Shapes!

I See Triangles

Mary-Lou Smith

Cavendish Square

New York

Published in 2015 by Cavendish Square Publishing, LLC
243 5th Avenue, Suite 136, New York, NY 10016

Library of Congress Cataloging-in-Publication Data

Smith, Mary-Lou, 1960- author.
I see triangles / Mary-Lou Smith.
pages cm. — (Shapes!)
Includes index.
ISBN 978-1-50260-224-4 (hardcover) ISBN 978-1-50260-223-7 (paperback) ISBN 978-1-50260-222-0 (ebook)
1. Triangle—Juvenile literature. 2. Shapes—Juvenile literature. I. Title.

QA482.S645 2015
516.154—dc23

2014032648

Editor: Kristen Susienka
Copy Editor: Cynthia Roby
Art Director: Jeffrey Talbot
Designer: Douglas Brooks
Senior Production Manager: Jennifer Ryder-Talbot
Production Editor: David McNamara
Photo Researcher: J8 Media

The photographs in this book are used by permission and through the courtesy of: Cover photo by Dave King/Getty Images; Pecold/Shutterstock.com, 5; Curioso/Shutterstock.com, 7; Digital Vision/Photodisc/Getty Images, 9; Jetta Productions/Iconica/Getty Images, 11; © iStockphoto.com/mg7, 13; Steve Heap/Shutterstock.com, 15; Jacob Termansen and Pia Marie Molbech/Dorling Kindersley/Getty Images, 17; Iurii Kachkovskyi/Shutterstock.com, 19; Pete Pahham/Shutterstock.com, 21.

Printed in the United States of America

Contents

Triangles are all around you.

All triangles have three sides.

You see triangles on **statues**.

The Statue of Liberty has triangles on her **crown**.

7

Triangle **signs** warn people.

This sign tells people to slow down.

9

Triangles make other shapes, too.

Arrows are made with triangles.

Some food is shaped like a triangle.

This grilled cheese is cut into triangles.

13

Slices of pie make triangle shapes.

How many triangles can you count?

15

This folded flag makes a triangle shape.

17

You can wear triangles, too.

The top of this hat makes
a triangle.

19

Triangles are fun shapes!

See how many triangles you can find around you.

21

New Words

arrows (AIR-owz) Shapes that signal a direction.

crown (KROWN) A kind of hat worn by a king or queen.

signs (SYNZ) Boards marked with letters, colors, numbers, or pictures to tell you something important.

slices (SLY-ses) Pieces cut from something larger.

statues (STAT-yooz) Objects that are made of rock or metal and look like a person, place, or thing.

Index

About the Author

Mary-Lou Smith likes to write books, crochet, and bake desserts. She lives in Boston, Massachusetts with her dog, Bagpipes.

About BOOK WORMS

Bookworms help independent readers gain reading confidence through high-frequency words, simple sentences, and strong picture/text support. Each book explores a concept that helps children relate what they read to the world they live in.